Little Pebble™

Habitats

All About
Rainforests

by Christina Mia Gardeski

raintree 🍃
a Capstone company — publishers for children

Raintree is an imprint of Capstone Global Library Limited, a company incorporated in England and Wales having its registered office at 264 Banbury Road, Oxford, OX2 7DY – Registered company number: 6695582

www.raintree.co.uk
myorders@raintree.co.uk

Edited by Kristen Mohn
Designed by Juliette Peters
Picture research by Wanda Winch
Production by Steve Walker
Originated by Capstone Global Library Limited
Printed and bound in China

ISBN 978-1-4747-4723-3
21 20 19 18 17
10 9 8 7 6 5 4 3 2 1

British Library Cataloguing-in-Publication Data
A full catalogue record for this book is available from the British Library

Acknowledgements
We would like to thank the following for permission to reproduce photographs: Dreamstime: Zaramira, 21; iStockphoto: ewastudio, 19; Shutterstock: asharkyu, 13, Dirk Ercken, 11, Eugene Huxley, 15, f9photos, cover, Kirayonak Yuliya, 9, Natasha Zalevskaya, rain forest design, Ondrej Prosicky, 17, PK.Phuket studio, 5, Salparadis, 7, Sergey Uryadnikov, 1

Every effort has been made to contact copyright holders of material reproduced in this book. Any omissions will be rectified in subsequent printings if notice is given to the publisher.

All the internet addresses (URLs) given in this book were valid at the time of going to press. However, due to the dynamic nature of the internet, some addresses may have changed, or sites may have changed or ceased to exist since publication. While the author and publisher regret any inconvenience this may cause readers, no responsibility for any such changes can be accepted by either the author or the publisher.

Contents

What is a rainforest?

A rainforest is a land of tall trees.

It is a wet habitat.

Lots of rain falls here.

5

Treetops cross.

They form a canopy.

Little sun gets in.

In the trees

Plants and animals

live in the trees.

Vines grow up the trees.

Animals climb the vines.

A sloth goes from tree to tree.

Frogs hide in leaves.

tree frog

The treetops are loud.

Parrots sing.

Monkeys howl.

On the floor

The forest floor is still.

Roots stick out of the ground.

A butterfly rests here.

Big cats hunt.

blue morpho butterfly

A crocodile cools off in mud.

Its jaws open wide!

Look up in the rainforest.

Look down.

Animals are at home

from top to bottom.

mountain gorilla

Glossary

canopy   treetops in a forest

crocodile   big, long reptile with thick skin and a long, thin mouth with sharp teeth

forest floor   ground in the rainforest

habitat   home of a plant or animal

parrot   colourful bird with a strong, curved beak who can copy speech

rainforest   warm, wet forest with very tall evergreen trees

root   underground part of a plant or tree that gets water and food from the soil

sloth   slow-moving mammal that lives in trees in the rainforest

vine   woody, climbing plant

Read more

Amazon Rainforest (Time for Kids), William B Rice
(Teacher Created Materials, 2012)

Poisonous Animals (Usborne Beginners), Emily Bone
(Usborne, 2015)

Secrets of the Rainforest (Shine-A-Light Books), Carron Brown
(Ivy Press, 2015)

Websites

www.activewild.com/facts-about-the-amazon-
rainforest/

www.ngkids.co.uk/science-and-nature/15-cool-things-
about-rainforests

http://primaryhomeworkhelp.co.uk/rainforest.html

Index